Book Level <u>5. 1</u>

AR Points <u>0.5</u>

GAME ON!

MINECRAFT

PAIGE V. POLINSKY

Checkerboard
Library

An Imprint of Abdo Publishing
abdobooks.com

abdobooks.com

Published by Abdo Publishing, a division of ABDO, PO Box 398166, Minneapolis, Minnesota 55439. Copyright © 2020 by Abdo Consulting Group, Inc. International copyrights reserved in all countries. No part of this book may be reproduced in any form without written permission from the publisher. Checkerboard Library™ is a trademark and logo of Abdo Publishing.

Printed in the United States of America, North Mankato, Minnesota
102019
012020

Design: Aruna Rangarajan, Mighty Media, Inc.
Production: Mighty Media, Inc.
Editor: Megan Borgert-Spaniol
Design Elements: Shutterstock Images
Cover Photograph: Gordon Wrigley/Flickr
Interior Photographs: Damian Dovarganes/AP Images, p. 15; Darren Worthy/Flickr, p. 17 (inset); Eóin Noonan/Web Summit/Spor/Flickr, pp. 23, 25, 29 (bottom); GDC/Flickr, pp. 7, 28 (top right); Jovial Joystick/Flickr, p. 22; Kevin Jarrett/Flickr, p. 13; Max Photography for GDC Online/Flickr, p. 16 (inset); Shutterstock Images, pp. 11, 16, 17, 20, 26, 28 (left, bottom right), 29; Wesley Fryer/Flickr, pp. 5, 9, 19

Library of Congress Control Number: 2019943321

Publisher's Cataloging-in-Publication Data
Names: Polinsky, Paige V., author.
Title: Minecraft / by Paige V. Polinsky
Description: Minneapolis, Minnesota : Abdo Publishing, 2020 | Series: Game on! | Includes online resources and index.
Identifiers: ISBN 9781532191688 (lib. bdg.) | ISBN 9781644942833 (pbk.) | ISBN 9781532178412 (ebook)
Subjects: LCSH: Video games--Juvenile literature. | Minecraft (Game)--Juvenile literature. | Mojang AB (Firm)--Juvenile literature. | Computer adventure games--Juvenile literature. | Video games and children--Juvenile literature.
Classification: DDC 794.8--dc23

NOTE TO READERS

Video games that depict shooting or other violent acts should be subject to adult discretion and awareness that exposure to such acts may affect players' perceptions of violence in the real world.

CONTENTS

Block Party 4

Indie Icon 6

Crafting a Company 10

Mod Madness 12

Mining with Microsoft 14

Minecraft Branding 16

Coders & Creators 18

Building Tomorrow 24

Timeline 28

Glossary 30

Online Resources 31

Index... 32

BLOCK PARTY

The sun rises over blocky hills. In the distance, square sheep and cows wander through grass. Your pack is full of tools and supplies. Will you search mines for gems? Will you build a cozy cottage? A giant city? In *Minecraft*, the choice is yours!

Minecraft is a video game developed by the Swedish company Mojang. Players enter their own worlds made of simple **3-D** blocks. Each world is **randomly** generated, so no two look the same. Players can break, place, or collect blocks. They can also craft blocks into items.

Minecraft has two main modes. In Survival Mode, players interact with in-game creatures, or "mobs." Some are friendly, like cows and sheep. Others, such as zombies and other monsters, are hostile. Players must fight off hostile mobs.

Creative Mode is free of hostile mobs. It offers players unlimited building supplies and has no rules or levels. Instead, players create their own experiences!

When *Minecraft* turned 10 in 2019, it had sold 176 million copies worldwide. It is one of the best-selling video games of all time!

INDIE ICON

Minecraft creator Markus "Notch" Persson never expected to design such a hit. In 2005, the Swedish programmer was working for the game studio King.com. There, he became friends with developer Jakob Porser. The two dreamed of opening their own studio. At home, Persson created his own games. He shared his ideas on TIGSource, an online community of independent or "indie" game players and creators.

In 2009, Persson left King.com and began working for the photo-sharing website jAlbum. In his free time, Persson was getting inspiration from the **PC** game *Dwarf Fortress*. In it, players gathered supplies and built structures. Persson began designing a similar game with **3-D graphics**. Players viewed the world from above. Then, Persson stumbled across a new game.

The PC game *Infiniminer* featured 3-D worlds made of blocks. Players gathered blocks, built structures, and mined for treasure. The **first-person view** made gameplay extra exciting.

In 2016, Persson received the Pioneer Award at the Game Developers Choice Awards. The award honors those who pioneer breakthroughs in gaming and pave the way for future developers.

Persson decided to give his game the same feature. He also made the **graphics** simpler and blockier.

After just a few days, Persson's creation was up and running. The single-player game featured blue sky, caves, and blocks of dirt and stone. Persson called it *Minecraft*.

Minecraft wasn't finished. But Persson wanted players to test the game as it developed. In May 2009, he shared it on TIGSource for others to **download**. Within minutes, reactions started pouring in. Players loved it! Within an hour, they were sharing pictures of towers, bridges, and other creations.

Minecraft became a hot topic on TIGSource. Persson used players' feedback to improve the game. A few weeks after he first shared *Minecraft*, Persson released a multiplayer mode. Players could now build together in shared worlds using **servers**.

To keep development rolling, Persson needed funds. In June, he began selling the *Minecraft* **beta**. Buyers were promised the future completed version for free. Within a month, Persson sold more than 1,000 copies!

In September, Persson introduced single-player Survival mode. Now, players had to fight off monsters! Gamers loved the action. With every **update**, their blocky worlds grew larger and more detailed. In January

REDSTONE POWER

Minecraft's redstone blocks can be used to create circuits in the game. Players have used redstone to build working models of calculators, computers, and even a Game Boy Advance **console**!

Minecraft players use redstone to build all kinds of mechanical structures, including roller coasters!

2010, Persson added crafting to the game. Besides stacking and breaking blocks, players could craft tools and weapons.

By June, *Minecraft* had more than 230,000 players. Persson decided to leave jAlbum. He told his former coworker Porser to quit his job too. "We're starting a company," Persson said.

CRAFTING A COMPANY

Persson and Porser had an indie hit on their hands. They released a multiplayer Survival mode in August 2010. By September, *Minecraft* had earned more than $750,000!

Persson hired business manager Daniel Kaplan to help start up the Mojang game studio. Soon, artist Markus Toivonen and programmer Jens Bergensten joined the team. Former jAlbum **CEO** Carl Manneh became Mojang's CEO in January 2011.

Though *Minecraft* had not yet been officially released, sales were soaring. That same January, the game passed 1 million copies sold. It hit 2 million in April!

In November, thousands of gamers flooded the first major *Minecraft* event, Minecon, in Las Vegas, Nevada. Minecon celebrated a major milestone. After years of testing, the **PC** version was finally complete. The crowd cheered as Persson revealed *Minecraft*: *Java Edition*. By the time of this official launch, the **beta** had already gained more than 10 million users!

Minecraft: Pocket Edition came out in August 2011. This mobile game was a simplified version of the original.

Persson was proud of *Minecraft*. But he was more interested in creating new games. In December, Persson stepped down from the *Minecraft* team. He remained at Mojang but turned his focus to other games. It was the end of an era. But *Minecraft*'s story was just beginning.

MOD MADNESS

Persson chose Bergensten as *Minecraft*'s new creative director. By January 2012, the game's community was full of talented creators. Players were even changing the game's **code** to create original content! Any changes to the game were called "mods."

Some mods changed the way the game looked. Others added new gameplay features. Bergensten encouraged players to design and share free mods of all kinds. He focused on offering better tools for making and using mods.

Mojang was on a mission to connect the *Minecraft* community. In May, the game became available on Microsoft's Xbox 360 **console**. Its split-screen option could support four players at once. Plus, the handheld controller made building easier than ever. *Minecraft: Xbox 360 Edition* sold more than 1 million copies in its first week.

Minecraft was also spreading into schools. Teachers were using the game to present material in fun, new ways. Students

Many school programs used *Minecraft* to introduce students to engineering, coding, game design, and more.

practiced foreign languages by labeling objects in the game. Teachers had students write histories for invented *Minecraft* towns. By September, a classroom mod called *MinecraftEdu* was being used by 250,000 students!

5

MINING WITH MICROSOFT

Mojang was determined to share *Minecraft* with players everywhere. By 2014, the game was available on Sony's PlayStation 3 **console**. Meanwhile, the **PC** version was selling an average of 16,000 copies a day!

In November 2014, Microsoft bought Mojang for $2.5 billion. As a small indie company, Mojang never expected to have more than 25 employees. Now, it belonged to one of the world's largest tech companies!

With this sale, Persson, Manneh, and Porser chose to end their *Minecraft* journey. "We're in it for the fun," Porser said. "We don't want to be a huge company."

Minecraft fans worried the game would change with Microsoft in charge. They loved the *Minecraft* community's freedom to create. Microsoft's Phil Spencer assured fans this wouldn't change. "We are going to maintain *Minecraft* and its community in all the ways people love today."

Microsoft's Lydia Winters presented the company's plans for *Minecraft* at a press event in June 2015. She showed the audience how *Minecraft* could work using augmented reality!

MINECRAFT BRANDING

Grass blocks, **pickaxes**, and hostile mobs called Creepers are just a few symbols of the *Minecraft* brand. Mojang features these symbols in its official *Minecraft* **merchandise.** It also licenses these symbols to other companies. For example, Mojang works with toy companies, such as LEGO and Mattel. These companies use the *Minecraft* brand to sell products.

Lydia Winters is Mojang's brand director. Winters creates promotional videos and hosts major *Minecraft* events, such as Minecon. She also manages all *Minecraft* merchandise! Mojang's licensing partners often present new product ideas. Winters decides if these products fit the brand.

Winters carefully reviews and approves every piece of *Minecraft* merchandise. She and a team of product designers study every finished product and package. They make sure nothing is out of place. "I can spot the smallest detail," Winters says.

The first *Minecraft* LEGO set came out in June 2012. Since then, LEGO has released many more *Minecraft* sets. They include "The Ocean Monument" and "The Zombie Cave"!

ADDING ALEX

Until 2014, *Minecraft*'s default player character was a male named Steve. When Winters joined Mojang, she decided the game needed a female character too. So Mojang added Alex, a player character with a ponytail.

17

CODERS & CREATORS

Microsoft was excited to support *Minecraft*'s creative community. *Minecraft* was introducing gamers of all ages to programming. But Microsoft wanted to do even more for young **coders**.

In 2015, Microsoft joined Code.org's "Hour of Code" campaign. Developers designed *Minecraft*-themed coding exercises for students and teachers. A coding tool called "Blockly" helped users work through games and puzzles. The project became one of Code.org's most popular coding exercises.

Meanwhile, *Minecraft* was in classrooms worldwide. By 2016, the *MinecraftEdu* mod was being used in more than 40 countries! Microsoft wanted to develop even more *Minecraft* tools for the classroom. In January, it purchased *MinecraftEdu* creator TeacherGaming. An official education edition was in the works!

Minecraft's developers were busier than ever. In April, Microsoft released *Minecraft* for the Samsung Gear VR, a virtual reality (VR) platform. Players felt as though they were dropped

The *MinecraftEdu* Treehouse Challenge helped students understand perimeter and area. Players used these math concepts to build the treehouses of their dreams!

right in the middle of the blocky action! Later, *Minecraft: Education Edition* launched in November. It bundled the best *MinecraftEdu* tools with free lesson plans and helpful apps. Microsoft also created a community program offering free teacher support.

CRAFTING FOR THE PLANET

Minecraft received an ocean-themed **update** in 2018. To celebrate, Mojang launched the Coral Crafters project. *Minecraft* players worked together to design structures that could support growing coral. These digital models were then constructed out of steel. They were placed off Mexico's coast to help coral reefs grow!

Minecraft fans gather annually at Milan Games Week in Italy. This industry event gives visitors a look at what's to come for their favorite video games.

By February 2017, *Minecraft* was home to 55 million players each month. As the community grew, so did the number of player mods. There were thousands of mods available. But it could be difficult to find quality mods that were easy to use.

In June, Microsoft launched the *Minecraft* Marketplace. It sold adventure maps, costumes, and other mods from top community creators, who received part of the earnings. "Our vision is to try and connect creators with our players," says Mojang producer John Thornton.

Microsoft's next big goal was to connect more players with one another. In September, the Better Together **update** united all Xbox, **mobile**, VR, and Windows 10 versions of *Minecraft*. Each platform now offered all the same items, gameplay, and Marketplace options. Millions of players could share one **server**!

The *Minecraft* community was growing nonstop. And Microsoft wanted to include everyone in major events. In November, it held Minecon as a free **livestream**. MINECON Earth was open to players everywhere!

LEVEL UP!

Since *Minecraft*'s launch, developers have continued improving and adding to the game. *Java Edition* alone has received more than ten major **updates**! "We're always striving to build and evolve the *Minecraft* universe," says creative director Saxs Persson.

2011

THE ADVENTURE UPDATE

+ New gameplay: players can mix potions, breed animals, and charm items; new Hardcore Mode locks game difficulty to "Hard," and players must delete their world after dying

+ Blocks and items: stone bricks, iron bars, glass panes, fence gates, chicken, beef, steak

+ New mobs: Enderman (tall, dark mob that only fights if attacked); Ender Dragon; Villager (human character that cannot attack or be attacked)

2013

THE UPDATE THAT CHANGED THE WORLD

+ New gameplay: user achievements added; "distance traveled" and other data now tracked

+ New places: Flower Forest, Deep Ocean, Savanna, and more

+ Blocks and items: stained glass, tree saplings, packed ice, grassless dirt, red sand, flowers, tall plants

Flower Forest

24

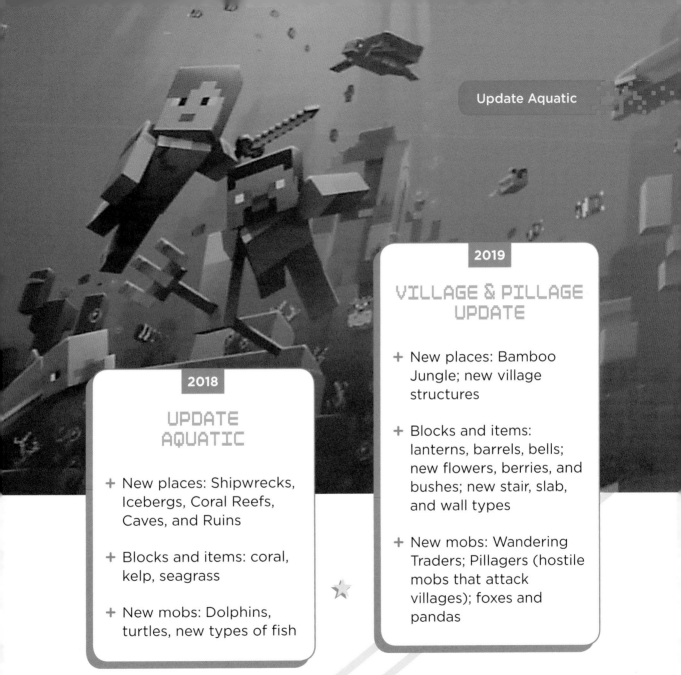

Update Aquatic

2019

VILLAGE & PILLAGE UPDATE

+ New places: Bamboo Jungle; new village structures

+ Blocks and items: lanterns, barrels, bells; new flowers, berries, and bushes; new stair, slab, and wall types

+ New mobs: Wandering Traders; Pillagers (hostile mobs that attack villages); foxes and pandas

2018

UPDATE AQUATIC

+ New places: Shipwrecks, Icebergs, Coral Reefs, Caves, and Ruins

+ Blocks and items: coral, kelp, seagrass

+ New mobs: Dolphins, turtles, new types of fish

BUILDING TOMORROW

By December 2017, *Minecraft* had sold more than 144 million copies. It was not slowing down, either. That month alone saw a record 74 million active players! In January 2018, Helen Chiang became the new head of *Minecraft*. She had plenty to manage. In fact, there was a new *Minecraft* title in the works!

In September, Mojang announced its development of *Minecraft Dungeons*. The multiplayer game would feature the *Minecraft* world in a whole new way. For starters, there would be no building! Instead, players would explore dungeons for treasure and fight off new mobs with up to four friends. The game would be released in the spring of 2020.

Along with developing new titles, Mojang continued supporting

MINECRAFT MOVIE

Mojang and Warner Bros. entertainment company will bring *Minecraft* to the big screen in March 2022. The **animated** movie will follow a group of adventurers fighting to save the world of *Minecraft* from evil!

Helen Chiang is the first woman of color to lead a major US gaming studio.

community content through major game **updates**. In 2019, Mojang was working on a project that it first announced two years earlier. The upcoming 4K Super Duper **Graphics** pack would feature clearer details and advanced lighting effects. This free

"I talk to so many people in the community whose lives have been changed by *Minecraft*," says Winters. "It gives people a creative voice to express themselves."

update would launch on Xbox One X and Windows 10 platforms. "We want it to be perfect when it comes out," Chiang said.

May 2019 marked ten years of building, creating, and exploring in *Minecraft*. To celebrate, Mojang released *Minecraft Classic*, a **web browser** version of the original *Minecraft*! Marketplace creator Blockworks also created a free map honoring the game's past and present. It featured a giant theme park packed with highlights from *Minecraft* history.

The next ten years have a lot to live up to. But Mojang has big plans. In May, it announced the upcoming test release of *Minecraft Earth*. This **mobile** game uses **augmented reality**. When players look at their smartphone screens, they see digital images within real surroundings. Players can interact with the structures, mobs, and items that appear to be in front of them!

No matter the project, Mojang's biggest goal is to bring the *Minecraft* community together. Markus Persson believes this community will always be the true owner of *Minecraft*. "It's belonged to all of you for a long time," he says. "And that will never change."

TIMELINE

2009

Markus Persson posts the first version of *Minecraft* on TIGSource.

2011

Minecraft: Java Edition is released in November.

2014

Microsoft purchases Mojang for $2.5 billion.

2010

Persson adds crafting to *Minecraft* in January. In June, he begins forming Mojang with Jakob Porser.

2012

Minecraft: Xbox 360 Edition comes out in May.

2015

Code.org features a *Minecraft* coding exercise for its "Hour of Code" campaign.

XBOX 360

MINECRAFT
XBOX 360 EDITION

7

MOJANG

2016

Microsoft purchases TeacherGaming in January. *Minecraft: Education Edition* launches in November.

2019

Mojang announces the upcoming release of augmented reality game *Minecraft Earth*.

2017

Mojang opens the *Minecraft* Marketplace in June. In September, *Minecraft*'s Better Together update unites gameplay on four major platforms.

2018

Helen Chiang becomes head of *Minecraft* in January. In September, Mojang announces the development of *Minecraft Dungeons*.

GLOSSARY

animate—to create a series of drawings, computer graphics, or photographs that appear to move due to slight changes in each image.

augmented reality—a technology that places a computer-generated image over the user's view of the real world.

beta—a near-complete version of a product that is still undergoing user testing.

CEO—chief executive officer. The person who makes the major decisions for running an organization or business.

code—a set of instructions for a computer to run a program. A coder is a person who codes, or writes these instructions.

console—an electronic system used to play video games.

download—to transfer data from a computer network to a single computer or device.

first-person view—a gaming perspective shown from the viewpoint of the player-controlled character.

graphics—images on the screen of a computer, TV, or other device.

livestream—the real-time audio or video transmission of an event over the internet.

merchandise—goods that are bought and sold.

mobile—capable of moving or being moved.

PC—a personal computer.

pickax—a tool for breaking up rock or ground. A pickax is typically made of a wood handle and a curved metal bar that comes to a point.

random—lacking a definite plan or pattern.

server—a computer in a network that is used to provide services to other computers.

3-D—having length, width, and depth, or appearing to have these dimensions. *3-D* stands for "three-dimensional."

update—a more modern or up-to-date form of something.

web browser—a computer program used for accessing information on the web. Apple Safari and Google Chrome are examples of web browsers.

ONLINE RESOURCES

Booklinks
NONFICTION NETWORK
FREE! ONLINE NONFICTION RESOURCES

To learn more about *Minecraft*, please visit **abdobooklinks.com** or scan this QR code. These links are routinely monitored and updated to provide the most current information available.

INDEX

augmented reality, 27

Bergensten, Jens, 10, 12
beta version, 8, 10
Blockworks, 27

Chiang, Helen, 24, 27
Code.org, 18
concerns, 14

developers, 4, 6, 18, 22
Dwarf Fortress, 6

graphics, 6, 7, 25

Infiniminer, 6

jAlbum, 6, 9, 10

Kaplan, Daniel, 10
King.com, 6

Manneh, Carl, 10, 14
merchandise, 16
Microsoft, 12, 14, 18, 19, 21

Minecon, 10, 16, 21
Minecraft Classic, 27
Minecraft Dungeons, 24
Minecraft Earth, 27
Minecraft Marketplace, 21, 27
Minecraft: Education Edition, 19
Minecraft: Java Edition, 10, 22, 23
Minecraft: Xbox 360 Edition, 12
MinecraftEdu, 13, 18, 19
mobile games, 21, 27
mobs, 4, 16, 22, 23, 24, 27
modes, 4, 8, 10, 22
mods, 12, 13, 18, 21
Mojang, 4, 10, 11, 12, 14, 16, 17, 20, 21, 24, 25, 27

PC version, 10, 14
Persson, Markus, 6, 7, 8, 9, 10, 11, 12, 14, 27
Persson, Saxs, 22
PlayStation, 14

Porser, Jakob, 6, 9, 10, 14

sales, 8, 10, 12, 14, 24
Samsung Gear VR, 18, 21
schools, 12, 13, 18, 19
servers, 8, 21
Sony, 14
Spencer, Phil, 14
Sweden, 4, 6

TeacherGaming, 18
Thornton, John, 21
3-D, 4, 6
TIGSource, 6, 8
Toivonen, Markus, 10

updates, 8, 20, 21, 22, 23, 25, 27

virtual reality, 18, 19, 21

Windows, 21, 27
Winters, Lydia, 16, 17

Xbox, 12, 21, 27